Also by Jill Krementz

How It Feels
When a Parent Dies

Jill Krementz

How It Feels
When a Parent Dies

Alfred A. Knopf   New York

19 🐕 88

THIS IS A BORZOI BOOK
PUBLISHED BY ALFRED A. KNOPF, INC.

Copyright © 1981 by Jill Krementz

All rights reserved under International and Pan-American
Copyright Conventions. Published in the United States
by Alfred A. Knopf, Inc., New York, and simultaneously in
Canada by Random House of Canada Limited, Toronto.
Distributed by Random House, Inc., New York.

Library of Congress Cataloging-in-Publication Data
Krementz, Jill.
How it feels when a parent dies.
1. Children and death. 2. Parent and child.
1. Title.
BF723.D3K73   1981   155.9'37   80-8808
ISBN 0-394-51911-6
ISBN 0-394-75854-4 (pbk.)

Manufactured in the United States of America
Published June 25, 1981
First Paperback Edition, March 1988

This book is dedicated
to
Dr. William J. Chambers
with my thanks

Contents

It was five years ago that I first thought about doing a book for children dealing with a parent's death. In July 1975 my friend Audrey Maas died, suddenly and unexpectedly after a short illness. What I remember most about Audrey's funeral—the indelible picture I carry in my mind—is her son, John Michael, then eight years old, standing there in the front row beside his father, Peter. John Michael was the only child in a roomful of grownups, all dressed up and trying to be very brave. Later at the cemetery he stood holding hands with his father, and once again he was fighting back his tears while the rest of us cried our eyes out. In the weeks that followed, my husband and I dropped by to see Peter and John Michael from time to time, as did many of their other friends, and I remember being told by a neighbor of theirs that John Michael often went next door to chat because he needed to talk to somebody and, more importantly, because he needed to get away from all the people. It seemed as though the influx of visitors, a comfort for Peter, was somewhat of an intrusion for John Michael. In any case, it was at that time that

I first started thinking about this book. And three years ago I started searching for the children who have shared their stories and their feelings in the pages that follow.

At first I felt very shy about asking children if they wanted to participate. But I soon realized that, without exception, the children I spoke with seemed to welcome an opportunity to reveal—and relieve—their feelings. The interviews were painful, but apparently the children appreciated it that someone was concerned—someone who was not a surviving parent or in some other close relationship to them. And this helped to confirm me in my hope that other children who have suffered the terrible loss of a parent might be solaced and strengthened by reading of the experiences and feelings of the eighteen children who "speak" in this book. Of course each child's experience is different from any other, and of course there can be no easy or simple comfort for the pain of a parent's death. But we all know how emotionally helpful it can be to realize that others have felt some of the same things we are feeling—the grief, the anger, the anxiety, the embarrassment. And I believe that within these eighteen personal and specific experiences there will be much that other children—and parents—will recognize and take comfort and support from.

One of the things I've realized while working on this book is that often a child whose parent has died doesn't know anyone else this has happened to, and feels particularly isolated and "special" in a very distressing way. I hope the book will help such children to realize that they are not alone—either in suffering so great a loss, or in the feelings they have about it. I also hope that many children will be able to read this book with their surviving parent and then find it easier to talk about themselves. Most of all, I hope the book will show children that there aren't any right feelings or wrong feelings; that acknowledging how *you* feel and not being afraid to express it is what matters—and helps—the most.

In closing I would like to thank all the people who helped me with the book—the friends, teachers, and librarians who introduced me to these children, and of course, most of all, the eighteen boys and girls who so generously and bravely are sharing with us here their most private selves.

Jill Krementz

Laurie Marshall, age 12

My father died two months ago in a plane crash. He was a sports-medicine doctor and he and a few of his associates were going up to the U.S. Olympics in Lake Placid. I found out about it around four o'clock in the morning. I had heard the dog all night. It was still dark outside, so I decided to go downstairs and see what was happening. The priest was in the living room and there were about four policemen. My mother was sitting on the couch, crying.

I thought something bad had happened. At first I thought it might have been a fire or a burglary, but then I thought that the priest wouldn't be there if it was a fire or a burglary. So I thought it had to be something worse. I thought something had happened to either my grandfather or grandmother because they're both getting on, but then I said, "What happened?" and my mother told me. I didn't think it was true.

Everybody was crying. The policemen left right away and some neighbors from across the street came over and sat with us. We let my younger brother sleep. Then around six o'clock the priest went upstairs to see if my brother was awake and he told him, "Something terrible has happened." Then he told my mother to come up.

I stayed out of school for about two weeks. I just wanted to stay around the house. It was around Valentine's Day, so a lot of my friends sent valentines. I think that's the way they wanted to say they were sorry, instead of saying it just straight out. It was easier for them, and for me, to say it on paper. The cards made me feel like they all cared.

We had a funeral and afterwards everyone lined up to shake hands with my mother. I met a lot of people that my mother and father had known. The funeral wasn't too long, so it was easy for me. I think if I had sat there for more than an hour I wouldn't have been able to take it. I don't remember too much. It's all mixed up inside me. There were a lot of people, all crying, with their heads down to the floor.

My father was cremated, but he hasn't been buried yet. That's because my mother isn't sure what to do. She wants to bury him behind our church so that we can go there whenever we want. She wants him to be close to us so we can go visit. And my grandmother, my father's mother, wants him to be sprinkled all over the farm, because that's where he was brought up. I kind of want him to be sprinkled over the farm more, because I think it's something that he would want to have done. And then we wouldn't really have to think about it and we wouldn't have to go visit him, so everything would be easier. I think that if he's sprinkled over the farm I can still talk to him the same way as if he was buried. I haven't talked about it with my mother because it would be just another big problem for her to think about and she's got so much on her mind already. It's just something else to cope with.

The other thing I'm kind of afraid to talk to her about is what really happened. They still haven't found out what made the plane crash. I have the feeling I want to ask her because she's been going into the city a lot and going to meetings and I think she might know something more that I'd like to know, but I'm kind of afraid to ask her because I don't know what she'll do, or what she'll say. She'll start crying. Not knowing what happened is terrible. It's like you're in suspense all the time and you just want to get the facts so that you won't have to think about it again.

In some ways it's easier for me that my father died the way he did—all of a sudden—instead of having to go through a lot of pain and suffering. The way I think of it is that someone good came down and picked him up because it was his time.

But it's still hard for me to believe it's really happened. Sometimes when I'm reading a book I'll forget and then all of a sudden I stop and remember.

My mother still cries a lot. I cried a lot the first month, but now I don't and my brother doesn't either. A few days ago I walked into my mother's room and she was cleaning out everything and she was crying. I tried to hold her. Some other times, before that, when I saw her crying I went in and started crying with her. It's made us closer than we were before.

3

The first time I went to school I was afraid how everyone was going to treat me because a friend of mine, Ingrid—her father died—she told me that her friends didn't know what to say, so they didn't say anything and so she was just kind of in a world by herself. Nobody would talk to her, and I was scared that's how it was going to be for me, but everybody just came up to me and started to treat me like nothing had happened. It made me feel a lot better because when people talk to me about my father dying it makes me feel worse.

When I do need to talk to someone, I usually talk to Ingrid. She's sort of like a big sister to me. She's sixteen and her father died two years ago, so she's gone through the same thing. She said the first four months are the worst and then it gets easier as it goes along. When my father first died, she came over every day and I told her everything I was feeling. It made me feel better to get it out instead of keeping it inside. It's better sometimes to talk to her instead of my mother because I don't like to make my mother more upset than she already is.

The hardest times for me are on weekends because we always used to go into the city with Daddy—to his office—and every once in a while he'd take us to McDonald's. Now my brother's hockey coach is always taking him into the city and doing things with him. Sometimes I don't think it's fair that he gets all the extra attention, and it makes me feel jealous and sorry for myself. He was probably a little closer to my father than I was, because he would go play ball with him and everything, and I'd be with my mother. So now he's getting almost everything he wants. I talked to my mother about it

4

and she said that she would plan some special trips for me, and that made me feel better.

A few days ago I was talking to my mother and she asked me how I felt about her going back to work and I said I didn't mind. I think it's a good thing for her to do because I worry about our having enough money.

And she asked me how I would feel if another man liked her and she liked him and they got married. I said as long as they're happy it was okay but that there'd never be a father like my father.

Jack Hopkins, age 8

My father died last year on Easter Sunday. He was twenty-nine years old. He had been real sickly for a while—dizzy and tired and aching in a way that made it hard for him to walk around. The doctor had told him to take some pills and stuff. So he was just staying around the house and relaxing. That's what he had been doing ever since summer.

I was playing a game with my three sisters in the living room when we heard a loud bang, the shot of a gun. My mother went into the room and she saw him lying in the bed. She screamed and told us not to go in there. We were so frightened about what had happened, and then she was on the telephone and when we heard her talking, that's when we knew for sure what had happened. We all started crying. Some policemen came over and the ambulance came and a whole bunch of people came over.

The last time I spoke to my father was about fifty minutes before it happened. I asked him if he could help me lift up my barbells and he said, "Yeah," but then he went back into the room and the next thing I knew he was dead. He must have known what he was going to do, because the day before he killed himself he paid all of his bills.

We buried him in his hometown of Thomasville, Georgia, because that's where my grandmother lives. That's a long ways from here. We went out onto the bank by the river and the minister preached some stuff from the Bible and then people who had flowers to bring put them on top of the coffin. Most of the stuff we heard made us cry, especially my mother and my aunt. I was just sitting there listening and trying to keep my tears back. It's the only funeral I've ever gone to.

I've been to the cemetery about five times since then. Once I brought a plant with me. It makes me feel better when I look at the gravestone because when I look at the words I can see his face. It says "Hopkins" and there's a pair of hands praying —like when you say grace before a meal. All of my family think he's in heaven, but I'm not sure.

For about three months after my father died, I didn't talk to anyone. I'd just go to my room and lay down and stare at the walls after I'd done my homework. Or I'd take a nap or just relax downstairs and do no talking. Sometimes my grandmother would call on the telephone and I'd talk to her for a few minutes, but then I'd just hang up the phone.

When my father died, we put his clothes in some boxes and put them up in the attic. I keep some of his colognes on my dresser for decoration. They remind me of him—the way he used to smell. My mother says that when I grow up she's going to give me some of his pens and pencils.

I still have dreams about my father. Sometimes I dream that I've died and my father's died and we're both in heaven and God just tells me why my father did this. My grandmother and my Aunt Theresa said that he did it for us, but I'm not sure that is true. I was just thinking it over last night and it might be right and it might be wrong.

I know he did it for a reason. I just can't say, "Well, why did the dummy do it?" or something like that. I don't know what the reason is, so I don't have any right to say, "Why did he do it?" I'm not mad at him. You just don't like to be mad at your own father just because he did something you didn't want him to do.

Since my father died, I've had to take care of my mother. She used to have backaches and stuff like that. My father would massage her back for her, but when he died I started doing it. I used to give my father back rubs too, so it makes me feel like he's there beside her. I have some extra responsibilities around the house—chores like trimming the hedges, keeping the driveway clean, mowing the lawn. My sister usually helps me push the mower because I don't have enough muscle to do it myself.

I don't really talk about my father very much. I talk to my mother once in a while, but I usually keep my feelings to myself. I don't want my mother to start crying because if she starts crying she starts coughing and stuff and then I get worried that she'll have to go back to the hospital. She's had kidney stones about four times, and when that happens we have to stay with Aunt Bessie or one of our grandmothers. So I worry that her kidney stones are going to get worse and

worse and the next thing you know—pop! There she goes too.

Sometimes I talk with my friends if they bring it up. When my father first died, they asked me how it happened and why he'd done it. That didn't bother me because I only knew one thing and that was *How* he did it, and I told them. *Why* I don't know.

We have family meetings about once a week and talk about anything that's on our minds. When he first died, me and my sister Cecilia we said, "Why in the world did they ever invent knives and guns and all that stuff? Guns shouldn't have been invented."

It's better for me not to think about it too much because when I think about my father I know there's nobody like him and I don't know why he did what he actually did. So I just say, "Jack, you might just as well relax and don't think about him and just live your life." So that's what I try to do. I can't say it isn't hard, because it is. When he first died, it was harder, but after a couple of months it started being easier on me. After about six months I felt a lot better and started playing again. I started getting more active and doing things I used to do when my father was alive. Like playing baseball. Only now I practice with one of my sisters instead. He could really throw a fastball—like you couldn't even see it, it went so fast. My sisters can't throw the ball as well, but they're getting better. And I like soccer better now anyway.

Susan Radin, age 13

My mother died seven years ago when I was only six. It was during summer vacation and the four of us, my mother, my father, my little brother, and I, were on a houseboat in France. One day my little brother fell overboard and Mom dove in after him. She must have had a heart attack or something when she hit the water. Someone else jumped in and saved my brother, but they couldn't save her. I mean, they got her body, but they couldn't save her from dying.

I don't even remember the funeral. After she died, I remember coming home from school and some little thing would upset me and I'd sit in the living room crying, "I want my mommy. I want my mommy." And when I had my second-grade birthday, it was weird because my birthday was on a Tuesday, but we had to have my party on a Saturday because that was my father's day off. I was really angry that I couldn't have my party on my real birthday.

Another thing that bothered me was that whenever we went to restaurants or museums or places like that, I didn't like having to go into the bathroom by myself. I would always feel jealous of my brother because he would have my father to go in with him. It made me feel left out.

My father got remarried three years ago to Miriam. They're both accountants and they used to work for the same firm. Now Miriam works for a bank. Even though I call her Miriam when I'm talking to her, I usually refer to her as my mother. I used to call her my stepmother, but then people would say, "What happened to your mother?" and I would say she had died, but then there would be like a void between us because my friends didn't know what to say to me. Another reason is because Miriam's parents didn't like it when I called Miriam my stepmother because they said it made their daughter sound like the wicked stepmother in "Cinderella."

I'm glad my father got married again because it's like having an appeal system. Like if my father says I can't do something, I can appeal to Miriam because maybe she'll understand. And sometimes it works the other way around. Also, I like Miriam.

I don't have too many memories of my mother. I don't re-member anything before I was three. In a way I wish I had more memories, but in another way I guess I don't want to remember too much. It makes me mad when people say, "I knew your mother for a really long time and she was a really terrific person." I feel I have the memories that I have and they have no right to tell me they have more. I don't know what to say to them. I've always felt that my own memories were very special.

When someone dies, they're considered perfect because you don't really want to remember the bad things—only the good.

It's like when you have a best friend who goes away to camp or somewhere. You don't sit around thinking about all the terrible fights you had. I don't want to remember any bad things about my mom.

I don't know where my mother's buried. I think it's in New Jersey, but I've never been there. I'll probably go by myself when I'm a little older. In a way I'd like to go there now, but I don't like to bring it up with my father. I think he was so upset by her death that he still can't talk about it. Last year during Yom Kippur I went to the synagogue. There is a special service called *Yizkor* which is when you say a prayer for the dead. Only people who have lost loved ones can go to the service. When I told my father I wanted to go, he understood, but I could tell it really depressed him when I brought it up. I think he wants to forget. I wish he could talk to me more about her, but I can understand how he feels. Sometimes I feel guilty that I haven't been thinking of my mother, but then I remember and I get really depressed. So like when I remember her, I want to forget.

We still live in the same house, so it's not that we're totally forgetting her. I wouldn't want to move. Like when I look up at the purple ceiling, I always think of her. We still have one of her favorite paintings on the wall, which makes me feel good. When she died, my father gave me some pearls she used to wear all the time. I don't want to wear them, I just want to keep them as a keepsake, along with a book she liked by Jane Austen.

My mother was religious and so in second grade I decided I wanted to go to Hebrew school, and I liked it. Last year when I went to temple for my Bas Mitzvah, there were a lot of times that I just felt my mother was there, supporting me and helping me. Every now and then—it just lasted a second, but I felt she was there. Occasionally I have dreams about her. Once I had a dream that she was lying at the bottom of a closet and she came back to life. When I have dreams like this, I just pinch myself on the arm to see if I'm awake or dreaming.

I do think that my mother can see me. Not always—it's just at certain times that I think she's watching me. Sometimes I try to talk to her. Like if I have a problem, I just think about it out loud.

Mainly I like to think about my mother when I'm happy. You know, if *I* were dead and watching people, I'd much rather know that the people who loved me were happy with their memories of me than that they were moping around and always asking why wasn't I back on earth.

Nick Davis, age 15

I remember the day my mom died very clearly. It was six years ago and I woke up and my dad asked me to go to the library with him because he had to do some research. We said goodbye to Mom and my brother, Tim, who was eleven, and off we went for the rest of the day. When we came back, we saw a big commotion about a block away from our house, and when we got home, Dad called out for Mom, but she wasn't there, so we went to a neighbor's house to see if he knew what was going on, and that's where Timmy was. The neighbor said Mom was at the hospital, and while Dad went there, Timmy told me what had happened. He'd gone out for a walk with Mom and there had been two taxi cabs that crashed into each other. One swiveled around and hit Mom and she hit her head—she was thrown up into the air against a mailbox. I didn't think that the accident was serious—I had this picture of Mom coming home that night with a big bandage around her head, telling some funny story about how it had happened. She would have been so good-humored about the whole thing.

A little later Dad came back to our neighbor's house and took us into the bedroom. He said, "Boys, I have to tell you something. Your mom died." There was a loud wail—really loud and really sudden. I remember hearing Timmy at the same time as myself. We went over and hugged Daddy and we cried for a long time. It was such a shock to me. Then Dad had to make phone calls to Mom's mother and to his parents, and I wanted to be with him while he did this. That night the three of us slept in Dad's room in his bed.

Dad said I didn't have to go to the funeral, but I wanted to. I would feel bad now if I hadn't gone. When I walked in, everyone was looking at me and I felt a strange sort of pride, like "I'm the one you have to feel sorry for." I know it sounds stupid, but that's the way I felt. I felt bad that Mom had died, but I also felt proud that everyone was looking at me, and I wanted to look strong. I didn't cry, because I had done most of my crying. The way I looked at it, there was no need to cry. There was nothing I could do to bring her back. There was no point in living in the past.

I was really mad at Mom. I never blamed the taxi drivers. I don't know why, but I didn't. I just took it for granted that accidents happen and it wasn't their faults but Mom should have known better. She should have jumped back more quickly like Timmy did. Timmy was mad too—mad that he hadn't been able to pull her back. He felt helpless that he couldn't help her, and that was rough. I even asked Dad, "Do you think Mom knows she's ruined our lives?"

Mom was buried out in Long Island and I've been there only five times. I've never been there on a sunny day, so it's always

been dark, and I've always been with someone who's crying. Everything there is ugly. Everything a cemetery represents is terrible—the way they look—orderly and gray, gravestones and slabs. Going there makes me feel worse. It just reminds me that people are going to die, and my worst fear is that *I'm* going to die. That's what I get out of going to a cemetery. When I die, they can bury me at sea or send me into space.

I'd rather remember my mother by thinking about her on her birthday and maybe going to temple on that day. I like it when people tell me stories and I get to know her better. I love finding out more about what she was like, because I was only nine when she died and I didn't know her that well. I mean, I knew her as a mother, not as a person.

Sometimes I see someone from the back who looks like her and I think, "Maybe she's alive and this is all just a cruel joke." I think maybe she's had amnesia and she doesn't know who she is and I'll go tell her.

Last year I read this story that I really related to. It's a horror story called "The Monkey's Paw" where you get three wishes. And this man wishes that his dead son can come back alive. Well, he gets his wish and the son comes back all mutilated because he died in some horrible accident. So the guy reaches for the monkey's paw and wishes him dead again. That's how I feel. I want my mom back, but if she did come back she'd be a vegetable or something. She just wouldn't be Mom.

About a month after she died, I once asked myself if it had to happen over again, would it have been better to have Dad die than to have Mom die. I didn't really answer the question because I felt so guilty about even thinking of it.

The first two years were the hardest. I still get a lump in my throat when I think about Mom, and I still feel bad. It's not as often as it used to be. Dad and I talk about a lot of things, but we don't talk about our feelings as much as we should. On the whole I'm closer to my dad than I ever was, and I know in some ways we couldn't get closer.

The thing about losing a mother is that now I know I can take just about anything. It was so painful, but I survived the loss and it's made me a stronger person.

Last year Dad got remarried to Karen and we're more of a family now. It's still a little weird to have people call up and ask for Mrs. Davis and it's not Mom. The first time it happened, someone called and said, "Hello, is Mrs. Davis there?" I never said, "Wait a minute." I said, "No, she's dead."

For a while I didn't think Karen had any right to tell me motherly things like "Wash your hands," "Eat your vegetables," or "Clean your room"—things like that. In fact, I still don't like it. I know she has the right to discipline me, but I prefer it when my father tells me what to do. And he's still the one I always ask if I want permission to go somewhere.

Jesse was born three months ago and he's a very unifying element. We can all relate to the baby. In some ways I'm his brother, but in other ways I'm just his half-brother. I'm his brother because we do things together and I take care of him. I'm his half-brother because I call Karen "Karen" and he's going to call her "Mom." I could never call Karen "Mom" and I sort of wish he couldn't either so that we could be perfect brothers. I wish that his mom was my mom and he would feel what I feel about Mom. As it is, he'll never know.

Peggy Laird, age 11

My father died about three years ago in a car crash. It happened so suddenly that everyone was in a state of shock. Sometimes I think it might have been easier for us if he had died from being sick because it would have given us time to prepare for it. Even now it's like he's not really gone. It's like he's just on a trip and he's going to come back.

When Mom told me that Dad had died, it was so painful that I could feel my chest hurting, like somebody had hit me. I screamed and I remember my sister Alletta screamed too and it was kind of like letting all the anger out.

A lot of people came over that day and they kept coming for about three days, but I wanted to be alone. Everybody was saying, "Oh, you poor dear. I feel so sorry for you. I know what you must be going through—here, have some brownies" —as if brownies would really make up for it. I got overweight from eating so much. I felt all the coming and going was an invasion of my privacy. It just made me feel more sad. I don't remember too much more about the actual day my father died except that it was the saddest day of my life.

Alletta and I both went to the funeral with Mom, but we didn't go to the cemetery afterwards. My little sister Irene stayed home because she was only two. I was only nine, so I didn't understand too much, but I had been to my great-aunt's funeral, so I knew what it was all about. Also, when my guinea pig died, we had a little funeral. We buried him in a shoebox.

Now that I'm older, I understand a little more and visiting the cemetery means a lot to me. It's a real pretty place. Irene named it Daddy's Garden and she loves to bring flowers there. I don't think I can grasp the fact that my father is really lying there underneath the ground. I think of him more as a ghostlike person floating around everywhere. And I do keep thinking that maybe one day he'll come back.

I don't like talking about my father's death too much because I don't want to feel pitied. I don't want my friends to say, "Oh, look at poor Peggy, her father died. We all have to protect her." I worry that they'll think I'm helpless, and I'm not helpless. I can do a lot of stuff and I'm not any different than I was before. There was one girl in my class who kept bugging me about it. I finally asked her to stop and she did.

The person I talk to mostly is Mom, but if I had to talk to someone else, it would probably be my English teacher, who's very nice. I can usually tell my mom what's on my mind even if she's the one who's upsetting me. For example, Mom got married again last year and for a while I felt a little jealous. After Daddy died, Mom was more ours—sort of like a mother hen with wings and all her chicks underneath. I was also having problems dealing with my new stepfather's children. I was afraid that if I got mad at them they'd tell their

father and he'd tell Mom and Mom would get mad at me, and my stepfather wouldn't like me and everybody else wouldn't like me. Mom said it was okay to feel jealous and that she expected all of us kids to get mad at each other lots of times.

In a way it's hard to be the oldest, because when you're younger and smaller, parents are more likely to take you up in their arms and hug you. Irene, especially, is always getting hugged. Of course I'm a little bit too big to be picked up, but if I'm crying, Mom will hug me and try to make me feel better. I want a little hugging without having to cry.

One thing that does help me a lot is writing in my diary. It's really neat because it's like a friend who will listen to you. I loved reading *The Diary of Anne Frank* because she wrote a lot about her secret feelings. Just like me.

Alletta Laird, age 9

When Mom told me that Daddy was dead, my knees started shaking. I almost fell down. My sister Peg screamed when she found out. My hands still shake when I think about my father. And sometimes I write faster than I normally do and it's not as neat as it should be.

I was worried that my mother might have to go to work and there would be somebody new picking me up at school all the time. I was worried that since we weren't making any money, it would make us poor or something. I asked Mom if we would go poor and she said no, that our family would help us.

At our school they told my class that my father had died, and it sort of made me mad because nobody ever played with me. I guess they were embarrassed. It's hard because they think you're different. I've never known anyone else whose father died, but if I did, I would try to cheer her up. I'd invite her over a lot. It would help if your friends could just play with you and treat you like you're a normal person. I would

prefer it if my friends didn't talk to me about it, but that's just how I feel. Someone else might feel differently.

Some of my happiest memories of my father are when he let me drive the bulldozer—I got to sit on his lap—and when we used to say prayers together at night before I went to sleep. Now I say prayers to myself. I don't have any unhappy memories because I don't count them as memories if they're unhappy.

I go to the cemetery with Mom when she goes to drop off flowers. She usually goes at Easter and Christmas. She took a rock which he liked and put it as a gravestone. I think it's very pretty. I didn't go to the burial service because Mom thought it would be too sad, but I sort of wish I had.

Last year Mom got married again. It's nice to have a man around the house. He gave me an electronic battleship for Christmas. We have lots of fun playing games together.

I still have dreams about my father—happy dreams. They make me feel good. And sometimes I see the light outside my window—it's on our garage—shining into my window, and I think it's Dad—his spirit. It's a secret. My mother doesn't know and my sisters don't know either. Nobody knows about it because the light only shines into my window. It makes me happy.

Stephen Jayne, age 11

I was eight when my father died. He was a producer for ABC News and he was going from Jordan to Beirut in a small chartered plane. There were only four people aboard—another producer and two pilots. The plane crashed right after take-off and everyone was killed.

I was in third grade and used to go home for lunch. A teacher came to my classroom to pick me up and I just figured she came because my mom wasn't home. So I went home, and my older brother and two older sisters were already there and they were all crying. I asked my brother what was the matter and he said something had happened to Dad. I went up to my room and started praying. Then a few minutes later my mother got home and told us Dad was dead and about the plane crashing.

The first thing I asked Mom was could we keep Skippy and Shadow, our dog and our cat, and could we keep our house, and she said, "Sure."

Our house was full of people who were trying to make us feel better, but they were all friends of my parents. So the next day I went over to my best friend's house. He took the day off from school so he could play with me. It helps if your friends treat you the same way as before your parent died. When they start feeling sorry for you, it makes you feel sorry for yourself and then you start crying.

We had a funeral in our church and all the benches were taken up and people even had to stand. So I knew my dad was important to other people. It made me feel good knowing that my parents had lots of friends.

Afterwards we went to the cemetery in a big black limo, and when we looked back, there was a long line of cars behind us with their lights on. There was an American flag over the coffin because my dad used to be a Marine. There was also a Marine honor guard, and after the priest said some prayers, two of the Marines folded the flag and gave it to us. Everyone cried a lot. That night on the evening news Barbara Walters and Harry Reasoner said a lot of nice things about my dad, and then ABC sent us a framed copy of what they said. We keep it on our living-room wall.

I stayed home from school for two weeks and when I went back I wasn't crying anymore. My friends said, "It doesn't seem like you're very sad your father died. It doesn't seem like you miss him." I did feel sad, but I just didn't want to cry in front of them, you know. One kid even said, "You must be glad your father died because you're not crying." That remark really got me so upset that I told my mom about it when I got home. She said it was because when they saw me, it made them all think how sad they would be if their fathers died and they didn't realize I had done all my crying at home.

I don't worry about money as much anymore, but for a while I used to go into every room and shut off the lights because I was so worried. And I was afraid to ask for anything special that first Christmas.

I hate it when people call up on the telephone and ask for my father. Like somebody who's selling magazine subscriptions will call up and ask to speak to him. If I'm the only one home, I'll always say something like "My mom's not here and I don't know anything about this and so can you give me a number and we'll call right back?" I don't want strangers to know my father is dead and think we're orphans.

The other thing that bothers me is when they make announcements at school—when the teacher says something like "I want you to go home and tell your parents such-and-such." I always feel embarrassed and I think everyone's looking at me.

My friends at school all know because the teacher told my class, but I don't tell other people. When I went to camp this summer, I had an ABC trunk, and when someone asked me about it, I just told them my father worked for ABC. I pretended he was still alive because they were all new friends. If I told them he was dead, it would be like going through it all over again and they would all have to say they were sorry. Everyone else in the bunk had a father, so I told them about mine so I wouldn't feel out of place.

Last year there was a guy who was taking my mother out and he was trying to help me in sports and stuff—like he came to

my soccer game. I didn't really let him help me because instead of thinking he was a friend I thought he was taking the place of my father. I didn't like that. Mom says I shouldn't have been that way because he was trying to help me a lot. Maybe I'll be nicer to the next guy.

I don't want my mother to get remarried, but I'd like having someone around who's a boyfriend to her and a friend to me. I don't want her to get married because then my mom would have a new last name. There's this other boy who's in the seventh grade and his mother got remarried. I was looking for his name in the phone book and I couldn't find it. Then I found out that the phone was listed under his stepfather's name and of course I didn't know his stepfather's name. So if Mom got remarried and changed her name, none of my friends could call me up anymore.

Another reason I don't want my mom to remarry is because everyone in our neighborhood says my dad was the nicest father on the block. If Mom married someone else, I think our friends would be nervous about being nice to him because they would think I wouldn't like it. Stuff like that.

I always imagine my dad as being super-great. Mom says I shouldn't remember him as being perfect because no one is.

I don't know if I'll ever see my father again. No one really knows about heaven because they haven't been dead yet. But I think part of my father is still with me. His body isn't, but his spirit is. If he's anywhere, I guess he's in heaven with my grandfather. At night I usually pray to God and say, "Please help Dad and Grandpop to have a fun time up there."

Helen Colón, age 16

My mother was sick for a very long time. She had multiple sclerosis before I was even born. She was paralyzed, but she could get around by holding on to the walls or pushing a chair, and she used to do therapy for her legs and stuff. So she could get around and she cooked and she was able to take care of us. I know I never really saw her walking because I remember once someone asked me how tall my mother was and I couldn't tell them.

My older brother Joe and I took care of her most of the time. I learned how to maneuver her wheelchair and since Joe was stronger than me, he helped lift her in and out of the chair. Finally she decided to come back to New York from Puerto Rico because the hospitals are better. So we came back and that's when everything got complicated. She had to have about six operations on her leg. My father was in the Merchant Marine and he stayed in Puerto Rico because he and my mother weren't getting along. My mother's best friend, whom I call Aunt Helen even though she's not my real aunt, lived in the apartment next door, so she helped take care of the three of us, my mother, my brother, and me. And we had visiting nurses who showed me how to help my mother with her exercises.

It was during this time that my mother got a urinary infection and went back into the hospital for a minor operation. It wasn't that big an operation, but everything was very complicated because if it wasn't one thing, it was another. She came out of that operation fine. But then her heart stopped and she just went into a coma. And she was in a coma for about six weeks before she died.

I was only eleven at the time, but I grew up real fast. I learned how to use the trains because I had to go visit my mother in the hospital. The doctors kept telling us that even if my mother didn't die the chances of her coming out of the coma weren't very good, and if she did come out of the coma she wouldn't be able to function because her brain was deteriorating from lack of air. So I thought it was silly when people kept on telling me, "You should talk to her, you should talk to her." You know, they say that when people are in a coma you should keep on talking to them and they might get better. I didn't buy that. I really didn't buy that. I felt very uncomfortable having to go over there and talk to her. I used to sit reading back where the visitors were supposed to wait, and I'd go into her room maybe once every fifteen to twenty minutes—that was it. After about three weeks of her being in a coma, with me sitting there reading, my mother's condition got critical and my family used to take turns sleeping at the hospital. I wasn't allowed to stay at the hospital overnight because I was too young, so I used to come in the daytime and stay all day. Then I used to go home and eat and come back. It was during the summer. I had just graduated from the sixth grade, and she died a few days before I entered the seventh grade.

I never thought my mother would die in the daytime, I always thought my mother would die at nighttime. And we got this call like at two o'clock in the morning and it was the doctor, who told my Aunt Helen. My aunt woke me up and she told me, and I remember staying in bed and crying. That's all I remember because everything just got so confusing after that with the funeral. Everything was just happening too fast. It was like I didn't have any time to think. I had to go along with everybody to do all the funeral arrangements. I don't know why I had to be involved. I would have preferred to stay at home.

I couldn't believe it, but we had to go out and buy a dress for her to be buried in. We went to so many stores to find one that we liked. And then I had to try it on. My mother was very skinny and I was very skinny, and so I had to try on a dress and make sure it fitted me, and if it fitted me we figured it would fit my mother. I pretended I was buying the dress for myself. We got a long one. I don't even remember what color it was. Peach or plum, I think. All I really remember is trying it on.

They kept the casket at the funeral parlor for a few days and every night I had to go there. I had to be around and I was really, really tired. I really wanted to go to bed. You know, if somebody dies, it could be so good just to be able to rest.

And I was so exhausted. All my relatives were sitting around eating and talking. That's what I remember most about the funeral. You know, family you've never seen in twenty years and they're all fussing over you and saying stuff like "Oh, I remember you when you were in diapers." You know, all that junk. I didn't like that. The only person I was really close to, besides my Aunt Helen, was my brother, the one who was sixteen, and he was in another world. He just sat there and cried and kept very much to himself. I really needed him, but he was too wrapped up within himself. I think the closest person to you is the person who can help you the most.

I didn't cry that much. I get carsick, so on our way to the funeral parlor I was too busy trying not to be sick. And at that moment it just didn't really hit me. I knew my mother was dead, but it didn't hit me until about four months later when I really started missing her a lot.

A lot of distant relatives stayed on after the funeral. Spanish people believe that you have these prayers every night in the home where the person died. They say the spirit is still roaming around in the house and will keep on roaming if you don't do these nine prayers. I think it's for nine days. I didn't know any of the prayers, so it wasn't doing me any good. My brother left to go back to school in Vermont and so it was just me and my father, who had flown in from Puerto Rico.

In a way I'm glad that my mother died when she did because she was always going to be an invalid. As it is, my childhood was shot. I mean, I could never go away to summer camp. Who was going to take care of my mother? I was very,

very thin because in the morning I would get up and make my mother breakfast. God, I was only nine. I had to make myself breakfast too, but I usually didn't bother because then I'd be late for school. Then I used to rush home at noon, make my mother lunch, and rush back to school. In the evening my aunt would make dinner, so I'd go over to her place, eat, and then bring dinner for my mother. She was a complete invalid. She couldn't do anything for herself. So I mean, if she were still alive, what would we have done with her? I would have had to spend the rest of my life taking care of her.

But that's my thinking now. Back then, no, I didn't want my mother to die. I didn't know what was to become of me if my mother died. My father and I didn't really get along. My mother was the only person I really had—and my brother Joe. It was just the three of us most of the time, my mother, my brother, and me. So when she died, I felt really sad. And then I started feeling angry—angry that my mother had died and left me. That's a biggie, you know. It's just like you feel you've been deserted. It's terrible, feeling that a parent has died and left you all alone. You blame them for a very long time. You think that it's their fault that they died and left you.

Sometimes I feel guilty too. I hate Saturday mornings because before my mother died I used to watch television— all the cartoons—and my mother used to ask me to make her coffee and I used to say, "Yes, later, later. . . ." She used to practically beg me to make her coffee, and so after she died I felt bad. That's the only guilty part.

We gave my mother's clothes to a real aunt of mine to donate to some church. I got to keep a beautiful eighteen-carat bracelet, and it's very pretty. And I've got a pair of earrings and a beautiful ring. It's like a wedding band, but my mother, like I say, was very skinny, so it doesn't fit me. I wear it around my neck if I wear it.

I also have two pictures of her, which I keep in my wallet. One is of her in Puerto Rico when she was young—she was about twenty. I got that from my grandmother. And the other is one that I took of her sitting in her wheelchair at my sixth-grade graduation. It just happened to be the year I won every award you could possibly win. I got all the medals. The only thing I didn't get was the spelling-contest trophy and attendance. I got everything else—I mean, math, English, and so on. I was also valedictorian, so I had to give a speech, and that was pretty neat. After she died, everyone kept on telling me, "You made your mother real proud before she died."

Even though I like wearing her jewelry and looking at photographs, I'm not sold on going to the cemetery. That's the worst place to remember her because I associate it with putting her into the ground. Why would I want to remember that part? My aunt's very religious and she's really into going to the cemetery and lighting candles in church and all that stuff. I don't think anybody should have to go to the cemetery. I can't see it. I think the most vivid thing in a person's mind should be the happy moments, and when you visit the grave you're left with the sad parts. It doesn't make sense. In the movies you always see the sad part where people go to the cemetery and they're all trying to relate to the person who died. It's all so unreal. I *cannot* relate to my mother by looking at her tombstone. It's hard to imagine there's a body under-

48

neath the ground even if I know it's there. The body's not that important to me. It's the soul that counts, and once that's gone, forget it. I wish my mother had been cremated.

The person who's been the closest to me since my mother's death is a woman named Mary Woodell, who is like my big sister. There's an organization called Big Brothers which has lots of men and women who want to be friends with kids who've lost a parent through death or divorce. I learned about it from a guidance counselor. He said, "You should call up this place so you'll have someone to pal around with." I just

called up and before I knew it I had an interview. My mother died in September and I got my new big sister in October. I think we got matched up because her mother also died when she was very young. We see each other every weekend and we do things like go to movies and go ice-skating. We just got into roller-skating this year. And we go out to eat a lot. That's something that we both love to do. And we go shopping. I have a big collection of stuffed animals. I guess they represent the childhood I never really had. But the best thing we do is just talk.

Meeting Mary is about the most wonderful thing that ever happened to me.

John Durning, age 15

My mother had been having really terrible blinding head-aches, and one afternoon when I came home from playing with my friends the doctor was there. Mom was in bed, and the doctor told me to go outside and wait for the ambulance. I remember it was in June because I'd gotten out of school— I had just finished third grade, so I was about nine. Mom went to the hospital and she stayed in intensive care for a few weeks. I visited her twice and then she got better and came home. Everything seemed normal and I went off to camp with Dave, who is one of my brothers. Then at the end of July another brother, Skip, drove up to get us. We were wondering why he had come a day early, and on the way home he told us that Mom had died from an aneurysm. At first I couldn't believe it, like "Whew!"—it was such a shock. We had a six-hour drive and all of us cried most of the way home.

The reason my father didn't come get us is because I'm the second youngest of ten kids, so he was home taking care of the rest of my sisters and brothers, especially my littlest sister, Jenny, who was only one and a half. She didn't really understand what was going on, but it was important for Daddy to be with her. When we got home, the house was packed with relatives because my mother came from a big family too.

The night before the funeral we all went to the funeral parlor and I spent a lot of time right next to her coffin. She was wearing a white dress, but that's about all I remember. I remember her more when she was alive because I think my mind wants to remember her alive rather than dead. I'm glad, though, that I got a chance to get a last look at her. I drew a picture for her and wrote a little note on it asking her to wait in heaven for all of us. I gave it to Daddy to put in the coffin with her, and even though she was dead, I like to think that she got that last message from me.

At the funeral I didn't cry much because I was too young to realize that I wasn't ever going to see my mother again. It was a real nice day and my brother Steve said the prayer and we all held hands around the grave. I know that what helped the most was having such a big family. Mom's death really brought us together and somehow we pulled each other through it. We had lost someone who was really special to us, and since we weren't going to get her back, we had to make up for it with each other.

I can still remember my mother vividly. I can hear her voice and I can remember how she would react to things I did. She never got mad at anyone and she didn't scold you—she just had a way of making you get mad at yourself. She could make people do anything, and do it well, because you'd make her so happy. And when you made her happy, it was so pleasant. Maybe it's just that I don't want to recall the bad

things, but I can't think of anything bad about her. She was
the prettiest lady I've ever seen in my whole life.

My little sister Jenny is so much like my mother it's almost
like seeing my mother reincarnated in her. She's great. I
know we all spoil her, but in a good way—she's not bratty at
all. It's just that we're all incredibly protective of her. She was
so young when Mom died that she doesn't remember too
much. Of course she's heard us all talk about Mom a lot and
oftentimes she and I will look at pictures together. She just
learns more and more, so even though she doesn't have her
own memories, she has everyone else's. It's very important to
all of us that she knows what her mom was like. Jenny's
probably the person I'm closest to now.

Tora Garone, age 10

My father died about a year ago in a hunting accident. He was out in the woods shooting rabbits and his rifle must have back-fired or something. It's hard to know exactly what happened. I was nine and a half at the time. My brother and I were away visiting my uncle in Texas and my mom called up and said we had to come home. She didn't tell us why or anything, and when we got home she told us the bad news. My father had actually died a week before we got home, but Mom didn't call us right away. She didn't want us to have to go to the funeral because she thought it would make it worse for us. I don't even know where my dad's buried, which upsets me. It would be nice to see where he is.

I wish I knew more details because it would help me get over it faster—I'd like to know just *what* happened and *how* it happened. It would help me to realize that it really *did* happen. I mean, I know he's dead because my mother had to send in certificates and stuff, but I'd like to know more. My mother thinks she's making things easier for me by not talk-

ing about it, but I want to know everything—even if it does make me cry.

I have a lot of nice memories of my father. I can remember the way his mustache felt when he kissed me. And I remember how he and Mom used to take turns cooking and he used to keep secrets from my mother—like he used to make this good chicken and Mom would say, "How do you do that?" and he wouldn't tell her.

The four of us used to do so many things together. We have a farm, so we would work together taking care of the chickens and the horses. We were very active in the 4-H Club and my parents were both 4-H leaders. We had a few horses and we'd all go riding. After my dad died, we sold most of the horses because we just couldn't take care of them all. My mother said I could pick one horse for myself, so I picked my father's horse. He's very gentle and I like him best. His name is Sheik. Sometimes I ride him in horse shows and I always try my best for my father. I think that if I ride him especially well, maybe my dad can see me—or something.

Meredith Meryman, age 15

I knew that my mother was sick, but I didn't know *how* sick. I didn't know she had cancer. I didn't think she would die. I just thought she had something wrong with her eye because she wore a patch on it. She was sick, off and on, for two years. She used to go for x-rays and sometimes she would have to stay in the hospital. But I always figured it was something she'd get over after a while. I never did know what really happened until afterwards.

The week before she died, my little sister, Henny, and I went to stay with Liz, a close friend of my parents, and her two sons. It was Christmas vacation and Mommy was really sick. She wasn't in the hospital, but she couldn't get out of bed and Daddy was busy taking care of her. One night while we were staying at Liz's, Daddy came and told us that Mommy had died. All I remember is that when he arrived I had a feeling that something really horrible was going to happen. We were eating dinner and Daddy said he wanted to talk to us. I remember going up the stairs with him and thinking something was very wrong. Everybody was very quiet and it seemed to take forever to get up the stairs. When he told us what had happened, it was such a shock that I just started screaming. Henny and I both did. Then the three of us went outside for a walk. The first thing Henny said was "Daddy, promise me that you will never marry again." That night I had nightmares about walking up those stairs.

The next day we all went to New Hampshire to be with my cousins. We stayed there for Christmas and I never saw so many presents in my life. Henny hated it that people were spoiling us, but I liked all the extra attention. The day after Christmas, Mommy was buried in Pennsylvania because that's what she had wanted, but we didn't go. Daddy decided that it would be better for all of us if we didn't go to the burial. He thought we were too young—I was ten and Henny was only eight—and he didn't go because he wanted to stay with us. So while the real funeral was going on in Pennsylvania the three of us went to Mass in a nearby church. Maybe we should have all gone to the funeral. I think it was nice of Daddy not to take us because I do think it would have been very hard for us, especially Henny. But I can't help thinking that it was kind of rude of me not to be at my own mother's funeral.

Ever since Mommy died, it's been hard for me to go to church every Sunday—the way we used to. I still go on Christmas and Easter, and sometimes I go and light a candle for her. But the one thing I can't understand is, if God's so terrific, how could He let my mother die?

We didn't take any time off from school, since it was Christmas vacation anyway. When we did go back, everyone knew what had happened because there was a notice in our school

newsletter. I felt, "Well, now *every*body knows" and it made me embarrassed and angry. I didn't think it was everybody's business. I don't think they should have announced it that way.

My sister and I reacted to my mother's death in totally different ways. Henny cried all the time and was constantly clinging to my father. She had to sleep with him at night. I was just the opposite. I blocked it out of my head. I didn't want to think about it. I wanted to get on with my life. The next day I was fine and I was laughing and playing with my cousins. And when I got back to school, I acted the same way I did before. I just felt a lot better by *not* thinking about it.

It probably was much harder for Henny because she was much closer to Mommy than I was. My mother was an artist and Henny is artistic just like her. Every day after school she'd go up to the studio and she'd draw with Mommy—or they'd go on drawing expeditions. I'd always stay home and do more things with my father. I was always Daddy's little girl. So when Mommy died, Henny wanted to be Daddy's little girl, and that was hard on me. She was so depressed that Daddy had to give her more attention and more of his love. I didn't want to cry in order to get his attention. So I yelled and screamed and was bossy and I took on the bad role in the family. I was always the one who got into trouble—who was doing badly in school—who wanted to be out with my

friends. At one point, I started wearing make-up and low-cut dresses. Henny was always wearing little lacy, frilly clothes, so I was more daring. Since Henny was getting all the attention, the best way I could get Daddy to pay attention to me was by picking fights and being obnoxious and mean. I've calmed down a lot since then. I'm still very immature, but now that Henny's more normal, I don't have to compete with her the way I did.

Last year Dad got remarried—to Liz, the woman whose house we were at the night Mommy died. I really love Liz a lot. She is so easy to talk to. I don't feel comfortable talking to my father about boys and stuff like that. Liz is also a much better

cook than Daddy. After Mommy died, we went through a year of burgers and spaghetti. Sometimes we'd order Chinese food, but it was burgers and spaghetti that we lived on. Liz also knows what to do if you get sick—like sticking the TV right in front of you and giving you soup and English muffins with butter on them. Once, just after Mommy died, I got really sick and the only thing that Daddy could think of was to give me some medicine.

I'm probably closer to Liz than I ever was to my mother. Mom and I were so much alike we were constantly fighting and screaming at each other. So in a way I'm relieved she's not alive now because I can imagine the fights we'd be having.

But in another way I'm sad because she hasn't seen me grow up or anything. I sort of miss having those fights with her because sometimes after you fight with your mother you feel closer to her, if you know what I mean. There are so many times I wish I did have a mother—like I wish I could bring a friend home and say, "This is my mother and my father," or I could just come into a room and say, "Hey, Mom, guess what happened in school today." I haven't said the word "Mom" for five years.

There are still special moments when I say, "Oh, God, I wish Mom were here." Like last summer our neighbors had a horse who was really scared and skittish around people. After a while he got to know me and he knew I was gentle and wouldn't hurt him. He would walk up to me and I felt so happy when this happened. Sometimes at night I'd sit on his back and look up at the stars and the moon. That poor horse had so many cries on his back and so many secrets told to him. He was sort of like my diary because I would always go and talk to him about what had happened during the day. I remember one night in particular, thinking how beautiful it was and telling him, "I wish Mom were here to see this." It's basically when I'm alone and happy with myself that I miss my mother the most.

Gardner Harris, age 16

When Mom first got cancer and was still at home, we all helped to take care of her, but it was my oldest brother, Amos, who did the most. He gave her her medicine and stuff like that. I didn't do that much, and now I really feel stupid that I didn't do more. Sometimes it became such a chore, which is a terrible thing to say, but it's the truth—and I guess I really couldn't accept the fact that she was as sick as she was. I was twelve at the time and it never occurred to me that my mother could actually die. Even now that I'm older and I can say I was too young or I didn't know how sick she was, I still feel guilty because I know I could have done so many more things for her than I did.

Toward the end she went into the hospital. They had strict rules about children visiting, so we couldn't see her every day. When she went into a coma, we still told her the news from home because we felt she knew we were there.

Throughout this time we all took part in family therapy. The house was in shambles, we were all going to new schools, and we needed help. A counselor came every week to see us and it was really neat. He just came over and we talked about our problems. He kind of prepared us for Mom's dying and he went to the hospital and helped her too.

Another thing that helped me a lot was that I was always going to church because I was in the choir. Whenever I took communion, I would say, "Please give some of this strength that I am receiving to my mother and help her get well." I was always hoping that she'd recover.

One morning around six-thirty I woke up because I heard Dad walking up the stairs. I'm not going to say that I knew what he was going to tell me, because I don't remember it that clearly, but I had a real strange feeling. Then he came into my room and hugged me and said it was all over. He only stayed with me for a while, which was good because I didn't want him to sit there hugging me. I wanted some time by myself to sort out the information—it was like somebody had died in the hospital far away, but that person was my mother and it was hard to connect the two. I didn't go to school because I didn't think it would be right, but it wasn't because I was overwhelmed with grief or anything because the information about the death of my mother didn't really mean anything to me at that moment. It wasn't like one of those scenes you see in the movies. I just couldn't realize her death until a few days later when I saw her dead in the open casket. That was one of her last wishes—to have an open casket.

When we went to the funeral home for the viewing, we walked into the back room and there she was, lying there with the light shining down on her. I walked into that room and I walked right out. Then I came back. I saw the shell of what had been my mother, but it wasn't my mother lying there. It was then that I realized that my mother had been using that body while she was alive, but that the real person, the person I loved who was Mom, was somewhere else and would never die. Her spirit was part of me and part of all of us. If I died and I had children, I would want to have an open casket too because it would help them realize that even if I died I would always be a part of them.

The next day we had the funeral and burial, and that was mainly uncomfortable because I didn't know how to act. One minute I was thinking I should cry, but then I'd say, "Wait a minute, why should I cry just because everyone else is? I *shouldn't* be crying, because I don't feel like crying." And then I wondered what else I should be feeling. It still didn't seem real. The viewing had made it more concrete, but it was still hard for me to get hold of the fact that my mother was dead, that she was forever gone. I kind of felt that her soul was all around. I felt like I was beyond crying.

After the funeral service we had the burial. When they were putting the coffin into the ground, I was especially glad I had gone to the viewing because I realized it was just my mother's corpse they were burying. There was no way that my real mother was really encased in that coffin. Then there was a wake at our house. All these people who were friends of my parents—people I didn't know all that well—came up to me and said how sorry they were. It all seemed so stupid to me that I just took my dog Shadows out for a walk. I didn't feel like being at a party.

Shadows was really great throughout that time. Whenever I was feeling sad, she would follow me up to my room and sleep with me on my bed. If I felt lonely, I'd just reach out and pet her. Crying has never been an outlet for me. I know it works for a lot of other people, but I do other things—like lie on my bed, or go out for a walk, or write.

Shortly after my mother died, I wrote down my feelings and felt much better.

What Am I: I Am My Mother's Spirit

I am my mother's slow-moving footsteps as she walks down to the hospital to get her cancer check-up, her utter despair as she finds the results, and her trouble in finding the words to tell Dad. I am the slow and reluctant boy who takes a couple of Mom's things to the hospital where she will stay before the operation. I am Mother's loneliness in her hospital bed as she patiently awaits Father's next visit. I am her joy to find us with him as he walks near her bed, her curiosity to learn of the day's events, and her sorrow as a very short visiting period ends. I am my mother's frail, ever-weakening body as Mom slips into a coma. I am the sparkling tear that runs down her stiff face as the words of a friend's letter roll out. I am the disbelief of everyone as the news reaches us that Mom has died. I am not the pounds of make-up that hide the painful expression on her cold, still face, nor am I her whole shell that lies in an open casket, but I am her spirit walking somewhere about the room. I am the sorrow of all as the casket is being lowered into the ground. I was my mother, I am her spirit.

I guess one reason I didn't want to cry was because Mom was always the person I went to if I was upset. I never went to my

dad. When I think about it, one of the real regrets that I had about her being dead was that she wasn't there to comfort me. But my biggest regret of all is that I wasn't around more to comfort her when she was dying.

Last year my father got remarried to a woman named Ann. After Dad told us they were going to get married, she came in and said, "Look, I'm no replacement for your mother. Your mother *is,* and I will be someone else. I will not try to be, and I will not want to be, and you will not want me to be, a replacement for your mother."

That was good because we were all able to accept her for who she really is. I liked her from the beginning, and now I love her. She's good for my father too, helping him to relax more and not work as hard. A few years ago he had some chest pains and I had a talk with him. I started crying and said, "Dad, you've got to stop smoking. You have to pay attention to yourself because we love you and we don't want you to die. There's no one else after you." It was so stupid of him to be destroying himself, especially since he was our last parent. Ann's a good influence on him and I'm grateful for that.

Carla Lehmann, age 11

My father died of cancer when I was eight years old. He was in and out of the hospital a lot and he was having a lot of drugs and treatments. Sometimes it seemed like he was eating pills and nothing else. When he was home, I helped take care of him a lot. I would fix the bandages around his leg. He used to lie on the couch in the living room and he liked to have his back propped up so he could see, so I fixed his pillows for him. And I brought him his food. And I watched him get worse and worse. That was the hardest part.

I used to hate it when he had to go back into the hospital because the first thing you think of when you're little is that hospitals are a place for people to die in. So when he would come home I always felt very relieved.

After about two years my father got really worse, so he went back into the hospital, and toward the end we didn't go to visit him because my mother didn't think it was good for us. I think she was trying to keep us from being hurt any more than we had to be because we had never experienced anyone dying before. But now that he's dead and I look back on it, it really makes me feel good that I was able to help him when he was sick—that he could count on me. It makes me feel as if my father is going to remember me now for doing all these things.

He was in the hospital for about two months and I remember it was just after my brother, Jackie, and I had come home from Vacation Bible School on Long Island that my aunt told us that my father had died. It was two days after it happened. My mother couldn't tell us. She was a real wreck. It was as if her life went off the track. Everyone was sitting around crying and I thought that if I cried hard enough he'd start breathing again in the hospital. In a way I knew crying wouldn't do anything, but I also hoped it would bring him back. Now that I look back on it, I know you can't just keep on crying all the time because it won't do anything.

I remember thinking that maybe his dying was some kind of punishment. I broke his typewriter in the office one time, and another time I broke his swivel chair and I thought it was as if I'd done all this bad stuff so, you know, his dying was like a punishment.

I don't think this anymore. I know he was really, really, really sick and that there was nothing that could really help him.

I also remember thinking, why was God picking on me?

It was like a bad, bad dream and I kept wishing I would wake up. And I felt so sad. I wouldn't talk to anybody for two weeks.

Lots of people came over to the house, but I didn't want to talk to anybody who had more memories of my father than I had. I didn't want to talk to anybody in the office where he worked because it was as if all these people knew my father better than I did. I felt very jealous of them.

Even the sympathy cards made me feel worse. I don't know why. They gave me a lot of strange feelings—it's like sadness and anger and blame and jealousy all mixed up in one. I was really mean after my father died.

And I was very worried about my mother. I was worried that she would die and if she did, where would we go? My mother explained that if anything ever happened to her, we would have to live with my aunt—my father's sister—and she's really strict, so this worried me a lot. But now I don't worry about that as much.

We didn't go to the funeral because my mother thought it would be too hard on us. But sometimes we go to the cemetery. It's about an hour's drive from our house—it's in Pennsylvania and it has pine trees around it and my father is buried next to my grandmother, way in the back.

We go there about once a year. It's pretty and very quiet. It's like walking into another world. Sometimes we have picnics there. It makes me feel better when we go there because I can really think there—I can really let my feelings flow. He has a pretty gravestone with a cross on it and two doves and a sun in the corner with the rays shining down on the cross. The doves are flying. We plant flowers and our grandfather also helps to take care of the grave and keep the grass around it growing good. I like going there.

My memories of my father are very important to me. I don't want to forget them because they make me feel better and also because if I have children I want to be able to tell them how it was. We used to go fishing all the time—he taught me how —and I got my picture in the paper when I was four and caught a nineteen-inch rainbow trout. It was really great. So I remember him whenever I'm around a pond—or when I'm camping, because we did that together. And I remember him when I'm with my dog, Princess. My father gave her to me when I was little and I've had her ever since. The other thing that I have that reminds me the most about my dad is a stuffed animal named Snowflake. It's a little white dog and he has a little red cap on his head with a little red pom-pom on the tip. My father brought it to me when he went to Michigan on a trip and I've had it since I was five years old. My mother used to keep asking me why I didn't get rid of it because it was such a mess, especially after Jackie pulled off the pom-pom. But I explained how much it meant to me and now that she understands she doesn't bother me anymore about it.

One thing that makes me feel sad is that every year at school there's a father-child night and Daddy always used to take me, so this is a real hard time for me now. I didn't go this year and it was like a part missing in my life. It was as if there was an empty seat there—and that night my mother went out, and that made me feel worse. I didn't say anything to her because I guess she's lonely and that's why she needs to see people. If she's having a good time, I wouldn't want to ruin that for her.

My mother has been seeing a man named John. He's divorced and his two children live with him. I hope they don't get married, because suppose they did and then John died? That would be really bad.

Another reason I don't want them to get married is because I know I would get mad at John for trying to replace my father. This year he took us down to Disney World and in a way it was fun, but in a way I felt sort of like my father would be mad at me because he always talked about taking us to Disney World and we always looked forward to that. So when we went with John, I felt that my father should be there. I didn't want my father to be mad at me for having a good time without him. I'm glad I went, but it made me feel very confused and it was sort of scary to me.

A third reason I don't want them to get married is because he has children and I know I'd have to share my mother with them. And since my father died, Jackie and I have gotten used to having her all to ourselves. Sometimes when she goes out with other people I just feel those people are trying to take her away from me.

I never thought about people dying before because you never think it's going to happen to you or anyone you know, but when it does, you think about it all the time. The only person close to me who died is my Uncle Jack—he was a close friend of my father's—and he died from cancer too. His daughter, Lisa, lives on Long Island and she's a year younger than me. We write to each other and whenever we see each other we talk about it. It really helps to talk to somebody who knows how you feel.

We all went to a psychiatrist for a while just after my father died—my mother, my brother, and me. We were all taking our feelings out on each other and I was having a lot of bad dreams—like my father's ghost would come back and haunt me for all the bad things I did. And my mother and I weren't getting along at all. So we went to this woman psychiatrist and she really, really helped. We saw her three times as a group and after those three meetings we stopped fighting a lot. We had all been so worried about the funeral arrangements and what we were going to do with his belongings— and it was just a crazy time for us. And I was so close to my father and I never thought my mother loved me—I thought she was closer to Jackie—and I used to keep all this stuff

bottled up inside me, which made us fight a lot. So talking it out was the only way.

It's hard to live without one of your parents, but I think you become adapted to it and after a few years it becomes natural. I know I can't sit there and daydream that he's going to walk in the door. Because I know it's not going to happen. I've even started doing some of the things that he used to do—like mowing the lawn, which is something I never dreamed I could do. And trimming the weeds and cleaning up the yard. And Jackie takes care of the garbage. These are things we feel real good about because we're doing something my father used to do and also because it makes us feel good about ourselves. Every year gets a little easier.

Thomas Joseph, age 14

I was six when my mother died. She jumped out the window from the ninth floor. She was visiting her mother when it happened. My brother and I were spending the weekend with my great-grandmother, so she was the one who told us. I remember crying a lot and my great-grandmother giving me a rag and telling me to just let it all out.

My brother and I didn't go to the funeral because it was at night. But I went and viewed the body. Before that, nobody had died who we were really close to, but my great-grandmother said to just look at my mother and then kneel down and say a prayer. So that's what I did. She didn't have a smile on her face. She looked like she was asleep.

My great-grandmother, she's real old. First she lost my mother and then she lost a daughter. I'm happy she's still alive, but I wonder why she is. I always expect older people to die first.

My mother had a nervous problem and I remember she used to go to this place called PHP where she could talk to a doctor and other people who had problems. My great-grand-

mother told me that my mother probably killed herself because she thought that after she died she would feel free and rid of her problems. And when I heard that, I felt much better. But I really didn't want her to die. I would have said that she should have coped with her problems—you know, try to deal with them, or get somebody to help her. If I had problems, I wouldn't just kill myself. I would try to live with them because I know I was put here for a purpose. I would try to deal with those problems.

I don't like to discuss my mother's death. When people ask me, I just say that my mother died, and if they ask me how, I say natural causes and sometimes I say cancer. If you say suicide, they ask you what kind of problems she had and what she did, and it just goes on and on.

I don't have too many memories of my mother because I was so small. I remember her taking care of the house and singing songs and most of all going to PHP with her.

My father tells me we have to work everything out together, since my mother's dead, and we have to try and keep this house together too—you know, doing chores. Me and my brother, Timothy, we have to wash the dishes and every other day we vacuum the floor. I don't like washing dishes, but then I think that I'm part of this house and I have to help keep it clean. It makes me feel better when I'm helping out.

I'm probably much closer to my father than I was before. And I know I'm closer to more people in my family, especially my father's mother. She's trying to help take the place of my mother. She's nice, but I wish my mother was back.

Valerie Crowley, age 15

My father was a fireman for thirteen years and before that he was a policeman. I always felt proud of what he did because he saved other people. He was like a soldier in a way, working for his country.

He died a year ago, after fighting a fire. He had come out of the building and was sitting down resting. Then when they were about to get back on the truck, he collapsed from smoke inhalation and had a heart attack. They revived him for about six minutes, but then he had another heart attack and died.

Even though he was a fireman, I never thought about my father dying. He never got a cold and nothing was ever wrong with him. Sometimes I would think that maybe he'd have an accident—like the rope would break or something—but I never thought he'd have a heart attack because he was always so healthy.

I was at my neighbor's house and it was about seven o'clock at night. My father's two good friends at the firehouse came to the door and said, "Your mother wants to see you." I didn't think anything of it—just "Oh, what does she want now?" I came home and the fire chief was there and so was the chaplain from our church and some other firemen. My mother was crying and she said, "Daddy's not going to come home anymore." At first I thought, "Well, maybe he just got hurt and he's in the hospital," because he had got injured once before. But then they were telling me that he had a heart attack and died and I couldn't believe it. I ran out of the living room and up to my bedroom. Then the chaplain came up and told me what a good man my father was, as if that would make me feel better.

My brother was only seven and I don't think he understood what was going on. He never even cried. He just stood there with no expression on his face. Even now, when somebody tells him he looks like his father, he'll say things like "What father?" as though he never had one.

Lots of people started coming over because as soon as they tell the family they can put it on the news. I didn't feel like staying home, so I went back to my friend's house and stayed there the rest of the evening. I called my fifth-grade teacher because I was really close to her—I used to groom her dog—but as soon as I said, "My father died," I started to cry and couldn't talk. She wanted to come over, but I told her I didn't want to see anybody and I thought it would be best if she stayed where she was. I just sat there crying and saying, "I can't believe it, I can't believe it," because he had died at three o'clock and that day at three o'clock I had been walking home from school with my friend and we were talking about

another fireman who had died. She had asked me, "What would you do if your father ever died?" and I had said, "My father wouldn't ever die. I wouldn't be able to believe it. I couldn't take it." It was really weird.

After it was on TV, I couldn't face my friends. I would walk down the street and they'd all look out the window staring at me. If somebody would say, "Hello," I'd just cry and then I'd run back home. I hated all my friends watching me on TV crying because my father had died, but in a way I wanted them to realize that he was a good person and that's why he was on TV and, in a way, famous.

Before the funeral we had a wake. That's when you go to look at him for the last time and you say goodbye. For me that was the hardest part. When I first walked into the room and saw him lying there in the casket, I was shocked because I realized he was really dead. Before they closed the casket, I kissed him on the cheek and got him all wet because I was crying so hard. I told him he couldn't go because I wanted to go with him.

I don't remember too much about the funeral because I was in another world. I just sat there and cried and didn't pay attention to things going on around me—a truck could have come through the church and I wouldn't have noticed. All my friends came and so did about five hundred other firefighters, but it really didn't register.

What I remember the most was seeing my Uncle Peter, my father's brother, after the funeral. They look exactly alike—almost like twins—and I was so scared when I saw him that I just gave him a kiss and ran up to my room and cried.

Going back to school was very hard because nobody would say anything. I guess my friends didn't know what to say because they felt kind of embarrassed, so they'd just look at me and no one would say hello. Then they started to be really nice and a few of the kids would say, "Oh, I'm sorry, I heard what happened," and I'd say, "It's true," and they all started sending me sympathy cards, which made me feel better. But it got to be a little too much—like no one would say the word "father" in front of me. So I finally transferred to a different school.

About a month ago there was a memorial service for all the families of the firemen killed in the last year. I went with my

mother and my grandmother, Daddy's mother. I know they were trying to make us feel better, but it just brought up more memories and made me cry. All it did was make me feel embarrassed because it made everybody feel sorry for me. I'm glad I went, though, because I like to see and talk to my father's friends. The best part was getting to meet some of the other families there. I had never met anyone whose father died the same way my father died, and when we started talking, it was as though we had known each other for a long time and we could talk so easily about what had happened. I like remembering my father, but I just don't like crying over him.

Sometimes I think that maybe my father didn't really die— that maybe they just told me that because he did something bad and had to go to jail or something. They say that time makes it better, but it hasn't really. It's just made me think about it more, and as time goes by, I think about him more, not less.

Sometimes at night when I'm saying my prayers and talking to him, it makes me cry. But if I hear my mother coming up the stairs, I'll stop crying right away because I don't like a lot of sympathy. If I want to cry, I'll cry on my own. By myself. I'd rather cry that way than cry on somebody's shoulder and get them all wet.

My father and I were so close—he was more like a friend than a father. Every Saturday we'd go to the firehouse and I'd go for a ride on the fire engine with him. Once in a while I'd help him clean out his locker and we'd usually have lunch together. Lots of times we'd go to dog shows together. And

we always used to take the dog for a walk together. Now that he's gone, I miss him the most when I'm doing the things that we used to do together. I can feel him with me when I walk the dog at night. And at dog shows I like to win because it always made him happy when I did. So sometimes I think, "This one is for you," and then when I win, it's fun because I think he's watching me.

I would like to be a fireman if they made it a little easier for women. My mother wouldn't be too happy because she says all firemen are crazy and it's just a way to end your life earlier. But I think that most firemen live and retire and it's like a brotherhood—they're all close to each other, like family, and they have a lot of fun. I like that kind of stuff and so did my dad.

Amira Thoron, age 9

I was only three when my father died, so I don't have too many memories of him. I remember his face and that's about all. We have lots of movies of him and I like to watch them. I used to think that if my father had to die, it was better that I was so young because I wouldn't miss him so much. But when my mother talks about him, it makes me envy her because she has so many memories.

I don't really remember much about my father. I remember strange things like getting up in the morning and climbing onto the foot of my parents' bed and Daddy waking up and saying, "It's too early, come back a little later." I don't remember his voice too clearly—just sort of. I also remember being at the dining room table and all of us eating hard-boiled eggs and Daddy reading the newspaper.

When my father died, he was cremated. They sprinkled his ashes in a pond near where we go for the summer. I'm glad they did that. It seems so terrible just to be in a coffin in a crowded old cemetery, if you know what I mean.

My father died of cancer, and for a while I was always afraid of getting sick. But now I know that I can't worry about it until it happens.

One thing that really got to me this year was one night I was at my friend's house and she hadn't seen her daddy for a really long time—he had been away on a business trip—and when he came back, everyone was really, really happy and he brought tons and tons of gifts and things like that . . . and it just kind of made me feel sad because my father wasn't coming back. He couldn't do that anymore because he was dead.

Sometimes my friends at school ask me how I feel about my father dying. And sometimes they treat me differently and they feel sorry for me. They say things like, "Oh, you poor thing," and it just gets me mad when people act like that. I don't exactly like telling people that my father's dead, but everyone in school knows. I mean everyone in the fourth grade knows.

Sometimes I pray, but it's only when I have to—like when I feel lonely or something, or if I feel really terrible, as if I'm the only person in the whole world. Or if someone is sick, or if I'm scared, or if I have a nightmare or something.

I used to be a real worrywart and worry that I was going to die. But now I realize that the most important thing is to have fun. There are so many things in my life I'd like to do that I just want to try and do them and not worry about dying. I'd love to be an archeologist or an architect or an actress and I'd like to go hang gliding. I'd also love to sail around the world and stop at a lot of places. I got this idea from a book I read about a boy who sails around the world alone and meets all different types of people. It sounded like a really good experience, but I wouldn't want to go alone— I'd like to go with someone who really knows how to sail. Daddy used to take me sailing and even though I don't have too many memories, I can tell from the pictures that Mommy has that I was really having a great time. It's really embarrassing because I'm naked, but I'm smiling from ear to ear. I love to sail but I'm not very good at it.

My mother has a friend, someone she's known for a really long time. He's sort of like a father to me. He's really nice and I don't mind if he treats me as if I'm his daughter. I really don't mind at all.

The thing I'm most terrified of right now is that my mother may also die. I've had a few dreams about her, of something happening to her, and whenever I have these kinds of nightmares I wake up crying because I'm so scared. This year my cat died and before that, my grandfather died and so did my mother's best friend. It just seems as though so many people in my family have died, and when someone dies, it's just like taking away a part of me, but I try to replace them with someone else I know. Now I realize that no one can last forever and I think it's made me a stronger person.

David Harris, age 15

When I first learned my mother had cancer, I felt sorry for myself, but then when I saw how sick she was, I just felt sorry for *her*. It was so painful to see her suffer, but in ways it prepared me for her death. I mean, it didn't hurt less. It couldn't hurt less. I was just able to withstand the pain more.

At the time, my parents were divorced and my older sister and I were living with my mother. But whenever Mom was in the hospital, my father came to stay with Sally and me so we wouldn't be alone. It was hard for my mother when she phoned and he answered, because she had been very hurt by the divorce. When my mother died, it was doubly hard because I lost her and I also had to move back in with my father, whom I didn't get along with that well. I suppose I blamed him in a way for the break-up. I went to a psychologist for a while after my parents' divorce, but I didn't like it. Counseling doesn't really help me. I have to work things out for myself. That's why I like being alone—just to think. If I can't solve a problem by myself, I don't feel I've solved anything. I keep my own counsel. I talk to myself in my head.

I knew my mother had cancer from the very beginning, because she never tried to keep it a secret. She didn't say, "I have to have an operation," or anything like that. After Mom's first operation the doctors told her that she had only a fifty-percent chance of living, and that's not encouraging, to say the least. She didn't tell me that part. I heard it from my aunt. My aunt was someone I could always talk to because she was completely honest.

My mother was sick for almost a full year, and toward the end—the last two or three months—she told me that she knew she was going to die. She could tell the drugs weren't working and she wanted to prepare me, if that was possible, for her death. I used to visit her for one or two hours every day in the hospital, and we talked about it a lot.

One time she said she wanted to die because it was so painful, but in a way she didn't because she wanted to be with me and Sally. I felt torn the same way—not wanting her to die, but wanting her to be free of pain. I knew that only one of two things could happen—either she would get better, which didn't seem very plausible, or she would die and stop suffering. Mostly I didn't want her to die, which sounds very selfish but it would have been like saying, "Oh, you can die because I feel you should be happy and who cares about me?" But nobody's like that. Nobody in the world is like that. I mean, I'm sure it's easier to commit suicide than to have someone you love die.

When the end did finally come, she was back in the hospital. On the day she died, my sister and I were with her for a couple of hours, but she was asleep the whole time and we finally left. She died about an hour and a half after we left. When I found out—my aunt told me—I guess I went into shock. I thought, "It's not real . . . it didn't happen." It wasn't real, but it was still terrible. I didn't cry much. I probably cried more before she died than afterwards. I suppose it was a consolation to me that she was no longer unhappy and in pain, but still it was like having the worst nightmare you could imagine.

Actually, it didn't register that it really happened until after her funeral. Until then I was just walking around like a zombie because even though I had been somewhat prepared, it was more on a conscious level. Subconsciously I could never really accept the fact that my mother was going to die. Subconsciously I was always very optimistic.

I'm still glad I knew how sick she was because even if it didn't make it that much easier, it did give me a chance to make the most of the time we had left. I got very close to my mother that last year. Before she was sick, she always used to want me to go hiking with her and do things with her and I never did because—I hate to say it, but—who wants to do something with a mother, especially if you're a boy and your friends are saying, "Oh, c'mon Dave, let's go bike-riding or skiing, or whatever"? It's hard to do something with your mother because they're stick-in-the-mud old fogeys. And the sad thing is that I didn't realize what it would be like *not* to be able to do something with her if I wanted to until after she couldn't do things like that. Actually, I did go hiking with her a couple of times before I knew she had cancer. We went across some of the White Mountains and we climbed Mount Madison. I had started doing more things with her because I realized I too would become an old-fogey stick-in-the-mud myself one day. But when she got sick, I guess I got closer to her because I paid more attention to her. I realized she wouldn't be around to be ignored.

I don't cry often. When I do cry, it's about stupid little inconsequential things, but that's a way of getting out my tears about my mother. I get really emotional when I'm frustrated. I think I've always liked being able to control the situation. For example, I've been playing Dungeons and Dragons for a couple of years now and most of the time I'm the referee. I prefer it to being one of the players. It gives me, you know, a certain power. I think I've always liked being in control, and usually if I set my mind to doing something, I can do it. When my mother died, no one had any control over anything. I am so incredibly bugged by that.

I haven't been back to the cemetery since the burial. This may sound like I'm not showing respect for my mother, but I don't think I could take it. It would be too painful to go there now. I don't love her any less if I don't go. It's mainly that if I don't think about it too often, it doesn't hurt as much.

It's been almost a year now, and it's strange—there are times when I miss her more than other times, but it's hard to single them out. I mean, I miss her a lot, but it's all on the same level. I did feel a little queasy on Mother's Day because I was with some friends and they kept on talking about their mothers. But I know I have to learn to take it because it's not going to change. It can't change.

I suppose my mother's death has probably made me more independent. I just have to rely on myself more. But a lot of my friends are also very independent because they don't get along with their parents—their parents don't like them and they don't like their parents—and that's had an effect similar to losing a parent. In some ways I'm more fortunate than some of them because I still have a parent who cares for me very much even when we don't get along. I think it's worse to have a parent who hates you than it is to lose one. Fortunately, my father and I are getting along much better than we ever did. He's still a pain sometimes and he still tells totally idiotic jokes, but we like each other a lot.

I hope my father doesn't get remarried. My mother was not the kind of mother you can replace. She was incredible. I loved her so much. I just don't think anyone could replace her and so I don't want anyone to try.

Gail Gugle, age 7

My daddy died nine months ago. It was at night when my brother and I were sleeping, so we didn't find out about it until morning. When we came into the kitchen, I saw Mommy crying. I said, "Where's Daddy?" and she said, "I have something to tell you. Daddy's been killed in a car accident and he won't be coming home again." At first we thought she didn't really mean it. Greg and I were both crying. We started asking her a lot of questions like how did it happen and where, and she said that he had been driving home from work and that his car had skidded on the ice. He had been working late, which is why we were asleep when it happened. Mom had gone to some friends' house to play bridge and Daddy was going to meet her there. A policeman went there and told her what had happened and she went to the hospital. By the time she got home, it was so late she didn't want to wake us up. Another reason she didn't want to wake us up was because she had to make a lot of phone calls to people like Daddy's parents. I remember hearing a lot of people talking, but I didn't know what was going on.

Mommy told us that Daddy's car had skidded on a patch of ice and crashed into a tree. He tried to control the car, but he couldn't. The police thought that maybe Daddy had been trying to avoid hitting a pedestrian or an animal or another car. I think this is probably what happened because my daddy was so kind-hearted he would have done his best not to hurt anybody.

We buried Daddy in Iowa because that's where he was born. First there was a memorial service in a chapel and the next day we had a graveside service for only the family. We put seven red roses on top of the coffin, one for each member of the family: Mom, Greg, me, his parents, his grandfather, and his sister. Red is supposed to be the color of love and the rose is supposed to be the flower of love.

We sat in some chairs and said a prayer and then we waved goodbye to Daddy. It was very cold, so we didn't stay for long.

When we came home to New Jersey, we had another memorial service. I thought it meant Daddy died again and I didn't like it, but Mommy told me it didn't hurt Daddy. It was for all the people who were alive so they could cry and feel open about their feelings. Lots of people from Daddy's office came. I guess I believe her, but it didn't really make me feel any better. It made me cry.

Greg is littler than I am and he thinks Daddy didn't really die —that he's in Italy or Iowa and that he's going to come back. He thinks it's a dream or something. Last summer when we came back from vacation, he thought Daddy would be in the house waiting for us when we came home. Greg says he misses Daddy most in the fall. That's because he and Daddy

used to rake leaves together and they would make a big pile and we would all jump in. He and Mommy do it now and Mom's getting pretty good at it. I like the jumping part.

I think my dad's in heaven. He's probably an angel. God tells him stories about me and then Daddy watches me from overhead. A neighbor said Daddy would come to live in our hearts so he would keep living with us but in a different way.

I don't talk about it too much. I talk to my mother and my brother, but I don't like to talk to other people because I don't want them to know about it. I don't want people to treat me differently. I don't want my friends to tease me. I would tell the class if Adam and Matthew and Michael were out of the classroom, but as long as they're not—no way!

Sometimes I talk about it with Uncle Mike. He's a pretend uncle who lives next door, sort of like a father to us now that Daddy's gone. He helps fix our bikes and we go jogging with him. He coaches Greg's soccer team. He's a good listener.

I think I miss Daddy more than Greg does because there's something special between daddies and little girls. I have more memories of him because I'm older. My dad used to come home from work and sit in the living room and play with us and throw us in the air or on the bed. We would tickle him. Sometimes we went swimming and I could always hear him say, "Don't go in the deep end." That's when I was real little. Before I was five.

Daddy and I used to go jogging together and on Saturdays we used to go to the malt shop and get a malt. After supper he liked to sit in his special chair in the living room and I always would climb on his lap and cuddle up next to him. Mom said when I was a little baby he used to sit in the same chair and hold me in his arms while he watched the football game. I love sitting in Daddy's chair on Saturday mornings watching *Mighty Mouse* and *Tom and Jerry*. Those are my favorite cartoons. It makes me feel that my father's just out working. I don't like it when other people sit in the chair besides me, because I don't like sharing my memories.

Special thanks to:

Rocco Staino, Eva Von Ancken, Christie Graham, Gene Young, Michael and Roland Harper, Beverly Selmeski, Sue Brooks, Tom Concannon, Dr. Stephen Summer, Jane Hansen, Judd Cohen, Shelley Emmer, and Barbara Abramo-Finkel, all of whom made it possible for me to meet several of the children in this book.

Janet York, Estelle Rubin, Karen Chitwood, Mary Wall, and Patience Moore, for their perceptive insights and general encouragement.

Carol Atkinson, who transcribed all the tapes after my interviews, and Valarie Hodgson, my secretary, who kept everything organized.

Erna Furman and Eda LeShan, whose excellent books dealing with the death of a parent were a wonderful help to me.

My husband, Kurt Vonnegut, for just being so nice.

And, as always, to everyone at Knopf, especially Bob Gottlieb, Martha Kaplan, Dennis Dwyer, Dale Demy, and Dorothy Schmiderer.

                                                                    J.K.